A Treasury of
Inspirational Thoughts

A Treasury of Inspirational Thoughts

S.P. Sharma

Publishers
Pustak Mahal®
J-3/16 , Daryaganj, New Delhi-110002
☎ 23276539, 23272783, 23272784 • *Fax:* 011-23260518
E-mail: info@pustakmahal.com • *Website:* www.pustakmahal.com

Sales Centre

- 10-B, Netaji Subhash Marg, Daryaganj, New Delhi-110002
  ☎ 23268292, 23268293, 23279900 • *Fax:* 011-23280567
  E-mail: rapidexdelhi@indiatimes.com
- 6686, Khari Baoli, Delhi-110006
  ☎ 23944314, 23911979

Branches
Bengaluru: ☎ 080-22234025 • *Telefax:* 080-22240209
E-mail: pustak@airtelmail.in • pustak@sancharnet.in
Mumbai: ☎ 022-22010941, 022-22053387
E-mail: rapidex@bom5.vsnl.net.in
Patna: ☎ 0612-3294193 • *Telefax:* 0612-2302719
E-mail: rapidexptn@rediffmail.com
Hyderabad: *Telefax:* 040-24737290
E-mail: pustakmahalhyd@yahoo.co.in

ISBN 978-81-223-0762-7

Edition: 2011

Printed at : **Param Offsetters, Okhla, Delhi-110020**

INTRODUCTION

This is not just another book of quotations. It is a book of inspiration—an excellent collection of sublime, inspiring thoughts and words of exalted wisdom.

Noble thoughts form the seeds of great deeds. Sublime thoughts of great men show us the path to an ideal and idealistic life.

This is a volume not to be read once and laid aside. To benefit from its contents, the significance of the ideas and ideals featured should be pondered over and integrated into one's life to the extent possible.

Besides, this treasury of wisdom highlights the aristocracy of the intellect and supremacy of the spirit and unveils the majesty of great minds.

The thoughts have been culled from a wide range of sources, Indian as well as Western, making this a truly universal compendium.

–Author

CONTENTS

SOME GREAT WORDS

The main purpose of life is to think rightly, act rightly and live rightly. The soul must languish when we give all our thought to the body. *– Mahatma Gandhi*

✳

Let us fill our minds with thoughts of peace, courage, health and hope for "Our Life is What Our Thoughts Make it". *– Swami Vivekananda*

✳

Knowledge is not something to be packed away in some corner of our brain, but what enters into our being, colours our emotion, haunts our soul, and is as close to us as life itself. *– Dr. S. Radhakrishnan*

✳

Education is not the amount of information that is put into your brain and runs riot there, undigested all your life. We must have life-building, man-making, character-forming assimilation of ideas.

– Swami Vivekananda

SOME PEARLS OF WISDOM

COMPASSION

If I can stop one heart from breaking,
I shall not live in vain.
If I can ease one life the aching,
Or cool one pain,
Or help one lonely person
into happiness again,
I shall not live in vain. *– Emily Dickinson*

✳

PURSUIT OF EXCELLENCE

If you can't be a pine on the top of the hills,
Be a scrub in the valley-but be,
The best little scrub by the side of the rill.
Be a bush, if you can't be a tree.
We can't all be captains, we have got to be crew.
There's something for all of us here.
There is big work to do and there's lesser to do.
And the task we must do is near.
If you can't be a highway, then just be a trail.
If you can't be the sun, be a star.
It is not by the size that you win or fail—
Be the best of whatever you are. *– Douglas Malloch*

✳

WILL

There is no chance, no destiny, no fate,
Can circumvent or hinder or control.
The firm resolve of a determined soul.
Gifts count for nothing; will alone is great;
All things give way before it, soon or late.
What obstacles can stay the mighty force
Of the sea-seeking river in its course,
Or cause the ascending orb of day to wait?
Each well-born soul must win what it deserves.
Let the fool prate of luck. The fortunate
Is he whose earnest purpose never swerves,
Whose slightest action or inaction serves
The one great aim. Why, even Death stands still.
And waits an hour sometimes for such a will.

– Ella Wheeler Wilcox

RELIGIOUS FAITH

I have enjoyed many of the comforts of life none of which I wish to esteem lightly. Yet I confess I know not any joy that is so dear to me, that so fully satisfies the inmost desires of my mind, that so enlivens and elevates my whole nature as that which I derive from religion-from faith in God. May this God be thy God, thy refuge, thy comfort as He has been mine.

– Lavater

COUNT YOUR BLESSINGS

Reflect upon your present blessings– of which every man has many-not on your past misfortunes of which all men have some. – *Charles Dickens*

✳

JUST TO BE NEEDED

"She always seems so tied" is what friends say.
She never has a chance to get away.
Home, husband, children, duties great or small,
Keep her forever at their beck and call.
But she confides with laughter in her eyes.
"Just to be needed is more sweet" says she
"Than any freedom in this world could be."

– *Mary Eversley*

✳

DO NOT PROCRASTINATE

Never put off till tomorrow
What you can do today. – *Chesterfield*

✳

QUOTATIONS FOR ALL OCCASIONS

ACCOMPLISHMENT

If you never take a chance, you will never be defeated, but you will never accomplish anything either.

– Anon

ACCOUNTABILITY

You can't run a society or cope with its problems if people are not held accountable for what they do.

– John Leo

A person may cause evil to others not only by his action but by his inaction too and, in either case, he is accountable for the injury. *– Joseph Addison*

ACTION

Do what you can, with what
you have, where you are. *– Roosevelt*

✳

ACTION AND INACTION

To act alone you have the right, never for its fruits. Let not the longing for fruits be the motive force of your action. At the same time, let not this stipulation lead you to persist in indolent inaction.

– *Bhagavat Gita*

✳

No matter how full a reservoir of maxims one may possess, and no matter how good one's sentiments, if one has not taken advantage of every concrete opportunity to ACT, it will not help in the improvement of one's character. – *William James*

✳

God requires a faithful fulfilment of the merest trifle given to us to do, rather than the most ardent aspiration to things to which we are not called.

– *St. Francis De Sales*

✳

Man does not attain freedom from action by abstaining from action. Nor does he reach perfection merely by ceasing to act. – *Bhagavat Gita*

✳

Surely none can ever remain inactive even for a moment, for everyone is helplessly driven to action by nature-born qualities. – *Bhagavat Gita*

✳

Perform your allotted duties, for action is superior to inaction. You cannot even maintain your body by desisting from action. – *Bhagavat Gita*

*

ADVICE

Advice is an uncertain gift. – *W. Jeffrey*

*

Advice is seldom welcome; and those who need it most, always like it the least. – *Chesterfield*

*

Action may not always bring happiness; but there is no happiness without action. – *Benjamin Disraeli*

*

Many receive advice, only the wise profit by it.
– *Syrus*

*

ADVENTURE

What a large volume of adventures may be grasped within this little span of life, by him who interests his heart in everything; and who, having eyes to see what time and chance are perpetually holding out to him, as he journeyeth on his way, misses nothing he can fairly lay his hands on. – *Sterne*

*

There are glorious years lying ahead of you if you choose to make them glorious. *–J.M. Barrie*

✳

ADVERSITY

Prosperity is a great teacher; adversity is greater, possession pampers the mind, privation trains and strengthens it. *–William Hazlitt*

✳

Adversity introduces a man to himself. *– Anon*

✳

There is no education like adversity. *– Disraeli*

✳

Prosperity doth best discover vice, but adversity doth best discover virtue. *– Bacon*

✳

God brings men into deep waters not to drown them, but to cleanse them. *– Aughey*

✳

Sweet are the uses of adversity. *– Shakespeare*

✳

AIM

If you don't aim at something, you will never hit anything. *– El. H. Christiano*

✳

AMBITION

The world makes way for a man who knows where he is going. *– Dryden*

✳

Hitch your wagon to a star. *– Emerson*

✳

ALTRUISM

When you are good to others, you are best to yourself.

– Dale Carnegie

✳

ANGER

Anger is temporary madness. *– Horace*

✳

For every minute you are angry, you lose sixty seconds of happiness. *– Emerson*

✳

APATHY

Apathy is the glove into which evil slips its hands.

– Bodie Thoene

✳

ART

A life of sacrifice is the pinnacle of art and is full of true joy. *– Mahatma Gandhi*

✳

Art is the stored honey of the human soul, gathered on wings of misery and travail. *– Theodore Dreiser*

✳

All great art is the expression of delight in God's work, not his own. *– Ruskin*

*

Art is collaboration between God and the artist, and the less the artist does, the better. *– Andre Gide*

*

ASK

Ask a lot of yourself, and you may be very pleasantly surprised at how much you receive. *– Anon*

*

ASPIRATION

Higher, higher will we climb up the mount of glory,
That our names may live through time in our country's glory. *– Moore (Aspirations of Youth)*

*

Ah, but a man's reach should exceed his grasp, or what's a heaven for? *– Browning*

*

The bird wishes it were a cloud.
The cloud wishes it were a bird.

– Rabindranath Tagore

*

Not failure, but low aim is crime. *– Browning*

*

Get up and set your shoulder to the wheel-what is this life for? As you have come into this world, leave some mark behind. Otherwise where is the difference between you and the trees and stones?

– *Swami Vivekananda*

✷

ATTITUDE

So often we seek a change in our condition when what we need is a change in our attitude. – *Anon*

✷

A BAD THING

A bad thing is dear at any price. – *Proverb*

✷

BEAUTY

Never lose an opportunity of seeing anything that is beautiful; for beauty is God's handwriting–a wayside sacrament. Welcome it in every fair face, in every fair sky, in every fair flower and thank God for it, as a cup of blessing. – *Emerson*

✷

Beauty is nature's coin, must not be hoarded. But must be current. – *Milton*

✷

There is no cosmetic for beauty like happiness.

– *Lady Blessington*

✷

Beauty in things exists in the mind which contemplates them. – *David Hume*

✳

BEGINNING

The beginnings of all things are small. – *Cicero*

✳

Well begun is half done. – *Horace*

✳

Every day is a fresh beginning, Every morn is the world made new. – *Sarah C. Woolsey*

✳

BEHAVIOUR

When you change your behaviour, you change your performance and you change your life. – *Anon*

✳

BOOKS

Next to acquiring good friends, the best acquisition is that of good books. – *Colton*

✳

The only real use of books is to make a man think for himself. If a book will not set one thinking, it is not worth shelf-room. – *W.L. Phelps*

✳

A good book is the precious life-blood of a master-spirit, embalmed and treasured up on purpose to a life beyond life. – *Milton*

✳

The true university of these days is a collection of books. *– Carlyle*

✳

And, books, we know,
Are a substantial world, both pure and good.
– Wordsworth

✳

BORROWING

Neither a borrower nor a lender be :
For loan oft loses both itself and friend,
And borrowing dulls the edge of husbandry.
– Shakespeare

✳

The borrower becomes a servant to the lender.
– Proverb

✳

Who goeth a-borrowing, goeth a-sorrowing.
– Tusser

✳

BRAVERY

Physical bravery is an animal instinct; moral bravery is a much higher and truer courage.
– Wendell Phillips

✳

True bravery is shown by performing without witnesses what one might be capable of doing before all the world. *– La Rochefaucauld*

*

The greatest test of courage on earth is to bear defeat without losing heart. *– Ingersoll*

*

Courage is the first of human qualities because it is the quality which guarantees all others.

– Winston Churchill

*

Courage consists not in hazarding without fear, but being resolutely minded in a great cause. *– Jerrold*

*

That enlightened one who is brave alike in pleasure and pain, he becomes eligible for immortality.

– Bhagavat Gita

*

Courage, as all true qualities, is a balance between extremes; its deficiency is the fault called pusillanimitty or faint-heartedness; its excess, disregarding the requirements of prudence, is rashness; if the excess endangers others, it is recklessness. *– Anon*

*

The courage we desire and prize, is not the courage to die decently but to live manfully. *– Carlyle*

*

BROTHERHOOD

There is such need for union,
Such need for clasping hands,
Yet we deny the brotherhood,
The human heart demands. *– Anon*

✳

It is not enough to struggle for the Brotherhood of Man. We must struggle for the Brotherhood of Living Creatures. Justice which does not include all forms of life, from tadpoles to whales, is not justice at all. Rather, it is a deal worked out between the members of a single, privileged elite.

Ancient people who worshipped animals, water wind, and trees, were closer to the Brotherhood of Living Creatures than we are.

If we do not return quickly to a state of harmony with the earth and reverence for all life, then we will in all likelihood perish. *– Bob Hunter*

✳

BUSINESS

I do not believe you can do today's job with yesterday's methods and be in business tomorrow.

– Nelson Jackson

✳

Business first : pleasure afterwards. *– Thackeray*

✳

CHANGE

God! Grant me the serenity to accept the thing I cannot change, the courage to change the things I can. And the wisdom to know the difference.

– Dr. Reinhold Niebuhr

✳

The world is the ever-changing foam that floats on the surface of a sea of silence.

– Rabindranath Tagore

✳

Even as childhood, youth and old age are changes of this physical body, so is death a change for the embodied soul. *– Bhagavat Gita*

✳

CHARACTER

The greatest hope of society is individual character.

–Canning

✳

When wealth is lost, nothing is lost.
When health is lost, something is lost.
When character is lost, all is lost. *–Anon*

✳

Character is destiny. *– Novalis*

✳

A man reveals his character even in the simplest thing he does. *– Jean de la Bruyere*

✳

Talent will get you to the top, but it takes character to keep you there. *– John Wooden*

*

CHARITY

Charity covereth a multitude of sins. *– Bible*

*

If you give what you do not need, it is not charity. *– Mother Teresa*

*

And now abideth faith, hope, charity, these three; but the greatest of these is charity. *– Bible*

*

Wealth is meant for charity–giving to the needy. *– Sankaracharya*

*

CHEERFULNESS

Gaiety is duty when health requires it. *– Anon*

*

Be cheerful! Do not brood over fond hopes, unrealised, until a chain, link after link, is fastened on each thought and wound round the heart.

Nature intended you to be the fountain-spring of cheerfulness and social life, and not the travelling monument of despair and melancholy. *–Arthur Helps*

CHILDREN

I do not love him because he is good, but because he is my little child. *–Rabindranath Tagore*

*

Every child comes with the message that God is not yet discouraged of man. *–Rabindranath Tagore*

*

If you cannot hold children in your arms, please hold them in your hearts. *–Mother Clara Hale*

*

CHOICE

I cannot choose the best, the best chooses me

–Rabindranath Tagore

*

CIVILIZATION

The true test of civilization is not the census; nor the size of cities, nor the crops, but the kind of man that the country turns out. *–Emerson*

*

The verdict on civilization will be:
Suicide while in a state of unsound mind.

–Dr. S. Radhakrishnan

*

Nations like individuals, live and die; but civilization survives. *–Mazzini*

*

Civilization is a progress from an indefinite, incoherent, homogeniety towards a definite, coherent heterogeniety. *–Gen. Edward S. Bragg*

*

COLOURS

Light finds her treasure of colours through the antagonism of clouds. *–Rabindranath Tagore*

*

CLEAN AND BRIGHT

Better keep yourself clean and bright; you are the window through which you must see the world.

–George Bernard Shaw

*

COME BACK

Four things cannot come back-the spoken word, the sped arrow, past life and neglected opportunity.

–Anon

*

COMMON SENSE

There is nothing so uncommon as common sense

–Anon

Common sense is the knack of seeing things as they are and doing things as they ought to be done.

–Calvin Ellis Stowe

*

Common sense is instinct, and enough of it is genius.

–H.W. Shaw

✳

Science is nothing but trained and organised common sense, differing from the latter only as a veteran may differ from a raw recruit. *–Thomas H. Huxley*

✳

COMPANIONSHIP

The companionship of the holy and the wise is one of the main elements of spiritual progress.

–Sri Ramakrishna

✳

Associate yourself with men of good quality, if you esteem your own reputation; for it is better to be alone than in bad company. *–George Washington*

✳

Avoid the man of temper, the selfish, the boastful, the scornful, the liar, lest you acquire his ways of thinking. *–Anon*

✳

COMPASSION

Nature never remains static; growth is essential for a human being. Why do we always say 'Happy Birthday' and never 'Happy Deathday'? Because we don't want to see the end.

The human mind is attracted to growth, beginning and freshness. Compassion thus is the force of growth and development while anger is destruction.

–The Dalai Lama

⁕

CONDUCT

Conduct is three-fourth of our life and its largest concern. *–Mathew Arnold*

⁕

The integrity of men is to be measured by their conduct, not by their profession. *–Anon*

⁕

CONFESSION

Confession of error is like a broom that sweeps away dirt and leaves the surface cleaner than before.

–Mahatma Gandhi

⁕

Confession is the first step to repentence.

–Edmund Gayton

⁕

Confess yourself to heaven;
Repent what's past,
Avoid what is to come. *–Shakespeare, Hamlet*

⁕

CONFIDENCE

Confidence is a plant of slow growth in an aged bosom; youth is the season of credulity

–William Pitt, the Elder

✳

Be courteous to all, but intimate with few; and let those few be well tried before you give them your confidence. *–Washington*

✳

By mutual confidence and mutual aid, great deeds are done, and great discoveries made. *–Homer*

✳

Skill and confidence are an unconquered army.

–George Herbert

✳

CONCLUSIONS

I have written of what I have seen and heard, but from the same clay two men will never fashion platters alike, nor from the same facts draw equal conclusions. *–Rudyard Kipling*

✳

CONSCIENCE

The virtuous mind, that ever walks attended
By a strong siding champion, conscience. *–Milton*

✳

Conscience is God's presence in man. *–Swedenberg*

✳

Conscience is the voice of the soul. *–Rousseau*

✳

Conscience is sacred sanctuary where God alone may enter as a judge. *–Lamennais*

✳

CONTENTMENT

When we have not what we like,
We must like what we have. *–Bussy-Rabutini*

✳

Sweet are the thoughts that savour of content.
The quiet mind is richer than a crown. *–R. Greene*

✳

Enjoy your own life without comparing it with that of another. *–Condorcet*

✳

CONVERSATION

It is all right to hold a conversation but you should let go of it now and then. *–Richard Armour*

✳

Silence is one great art of conversation.
–William Hazlitt

✳

COURTESY

The small courtesies sweeten life, the greater, ennoble it.
–Bovee

✳

CREDIT

The way to get things done is not to mind who gets the credit for doing them. *–Benjamin Jowett*

✳

A creditor is worse than a master; for a master owns only your person, a creditor owns your dignity, and can belabour that. *–Victor Hugo*

✳

CRITICISM

The trouble with most of us is that we would rather be ruined by praise than be saved by criticism.
–Anon

✳

CULTURE

No culture can live if it attempts to be exclusive.
–Mahatma Gandhi

✳

Culture, first of all, is not loud; it is quiet, it is tolerant, it is restrained. You may judge the culture of a person by his silence, by a gesture, by a phrase, more specially, by his life generally. *–Jawaharlal Nehru*

✳

Culture is "to know the best that has been said and thought in the world." *–Mathew Arnold*

✳

Culture is the passion for sweetness and light.

–Mathew Arnold

✳

DANGER

It is idle to expect that dangers and difficulties will not come. But, for a devotee, they will pass away from under the feet like water. *–Sri Saradamani Devi*

✳

We triumph without glory when we conquer without danger. *–Corneille*

✳

Danger, the spur of all great minds.

–George Chapman

✳

Out of this nettle, danger,
We pluck this flower, safety. *–Shakespeare*

✳

DARKNESS

We are not here to curse the darkness, but to light the candle that can guide us through the darkness to a safe and sane future. *–John Kennedy*

✳

Darkness travels towards light but blindness towards death. *–Rabindranath Tagore*

✻

It is always darkest just before the day dawneth.

–Thomas Fuller

✻

DEATH

Both of them are ignorant: he who thinks the soul to be capable of killing and who takes it as killed, for the soul knows no death.

As a man shedding worn-out garments, takes on new ones, the embodied soul, casting off worn out bodies, enters into others which are new.

Death is certain for the born and rebirth inevitable for the dead. You should not grieve over the inevitable. *–Bhagavat Gita*

✻

The undiscovered country, from whose bourn,
No traveller returns. *–Shakespeare*

✻

Death's stamp gives value to the coin of life; making it possible to buy with life what is truly precious.

–Rabindranath Tagore

✻

The fountain of death makes the still water play.

–Rabindranath Tagore

DEFECTS

It is in general more profitable to reckon up our defects than to boast of our attainments. *–Carlyle*

There are persons who ponder upon the shortcomings of their friends. There is nothing to be gained by this. I have always paid attention to the merit of my adversaries, and have derived advantages from doing so. *–Goethe*

DESPAIR

Never despair. But if you do, work in despair.

–Edmund Burke

Despair doubles our strength. *–Proverb*

DEVOTION

O, son of Kunti! whatever you do, whatever you eat, whatever you offer in sacrifice, whatever you give in charity, whatever austerity you perform-do that as offering unto Me. *–Lord Krishna in Bhagavat Gita*

The devotees who loving me exclusively, constantly think of me and worship me, to such steadfast devotees, I bring full security and personally provide for all their needs. *–Lord Krishna in Bhagavat Gita*

✳

The self-controlled aspirant, while enjoying the various sense-objects through his senses, which are disciplined and detached, attains complete tranquillity of mind.

How can there be happiness, peace of mind for one who is not tranquil? *–Lord Krishna in Bhagavat Gita*

*

DHARMA

Dharma violated destroys,
Dharma cherished protects. *–Mahabharata*

*

That which is conducive to the welfare of beings is surely dharma, as dharma has been propounded for the welfare of beings.

That which is conducive to 'ahimsa' (non-injuriousness) is surely dharma for dharma is propounded to protect beings from violence (ahimsa).

–Dharmasastras

He who is always the friend of all, and who through thought, word and deed, is absorbed in promoting the welfare of all, knows what is dharma.

–Mahabharata

DIFFICULTY

Smooth seas do not make skilful sailors. *–Proverb*

Many things difficult to design prove easy to perform.
–Samuel Johnson

*

The best way out of a difficulty is through it. *–Anon*

*

Difficulty is a severe instructor. *–Burke*

*

DISCIPLINE

Discipline is a process of scheduling the pain and pleasure of life in such a way as to enhance the pleasure by meeting and experiencing the pain first and getting over with it. *–Dr M. Scott Peck*

When the method and discipline of knowledge are added to talent, the result is altogether outstanding.
–Cicero

The secret of such commitment is getting past the drudgery and seeing the delight. "The fact is that many worthwhile endeavours are not fun.

True, all work and no play makes Jack a dull boy. But trying to turn everything we do into play makes for terrible frustrations, because life, even the most rewarding one, includes circumstances that are not fun at all". *–Anon*

Discipline is the refining fire by which talent becomes ability. *–Roy Smith*

✷

Disciplined people are happier people because they are fulfilling inner potential. True discipline achieves a balance of producing, but not pushing; of diligence, not driving. Even discipline needs to be disciplined.

–Anon

✷

Discipline is habit-forming. A little leads to more, because the benefits prove increasingly desirable. When you finally overcome inertia, you will feel better all round. We are at our best, physically and mentally, when we are disciplined. *–Sybil Stanton*

✷

DISCOVERY

Discovery consists of seeing what everybody has seen and thinking what nobody has thought.

–A.S. Gyorgyi

✷

All really big discoveries are the result of thought patiently pursued. *–Alexander Graham Bell*

✷

Don't keep forever on the public road, going only where others have gone, and following after one another like a flock of sheep.

Leave the beaten track occasionally, and dive into the woods. Every time you do so, you will be certain to see something that you have never seen before.

Of course, it will be a little thing, but do not ignore it. Follow it up, explore all around it, one discovery will lead to another and before you know it, you will have something worth thinking about to occupy your mind. *–Alexander Graham Bell*

✳

It does seem a little strange that while some people get discovered, others just get found out.

–Paul C. Hody

✳

DIVINITY

Each soul is potentially divine. The goal is to manifest this divinity within by controlling nature, external and internal. *–Swami Vivekananda*

✳

There is a divinity that shapes our ends.
Rough-hew them how we will. *–Shakespeare*

✳

DOING OUR BEST

Let me but do my work from day to day,
In field or forest, at the desk or loom,
In roaring market place or tranquil room;

Let me but find it in my heart to say, when vagrant wishes beckon me astray,
"This is my work; my blessing, not my doom,
Of all who live, I am the one by whom,
This work can best be done in the right way".

Then shall I see it not too great, nor small,
To suit my spirit and to prove my powers;
Then shall I cheerful greet the labouring hours,
And cheerful turn, when the long shadows fall
At eventide, to play and love and rest,
Because I know for me my work is best.

–Henry Van Dyke

✳

DOUBTS

Our doubts are traitors,
And make us lose the good we oft might win,
By fearing to attempt. *–Shakespeare*

✳

The doubting man perishes. *–Bhagavat Gita*

✳

He who never doubts does not know anything.

–Proverb

✳

DREAMS

Some people look at things as they are and ask why. We dream things as they never were and ask why not. *–Robert Kennedy*

✳

If one advances confidently in the direction of his dreams and endeavours to live the life which he has imagined, he will meet with a success unexpected in common hours... If you have built castles in the air, your work need not be lost; that is where they should be. Now put the foundation under them.

–Henry David Thoreau

✳

DUTY

Speed is not the end of life. Man sees more and lives more truly by walking to his duty.

–Mahatma Gandhi

✳

Make it a point to do something every day that you don't want to do. This is the golden rule for acquiring the habit of doing your duty without pain.

–Mark Twain

✳

The little that has been done should not blind us to the vast that remains to be done.

–Dr. S. Radhakrishnan

✳

The path of duty is the way to glory. *–Tennyson*

✳

Truth is a divine word. Duty is divine law.

–D.C. Mackintosh

✳

One's own duty though appears to be mundane, is preferable to the duty of another, well performed. Even death in the performance of one's own duty brings blessedness another's duty is fraught with danger of downfall. *–Bhagavat Gita*

*

EARNESTNESS

Earnestness is enthusiasm tempered by reason.

–Blaise Pascal

*

EDUCATION

Education, to be complete, must be humane; it must include not only the training of the intellect but also the refinement of the heart and the discipline of the spirit. *–Dr. S. Radhakrishnan*

*

What sculpture is to a piece of marble, education is to the soul. *–Joseph Addison*

*

The ink of the scholar is more holy than the blood of the martyr. *–Koran*

*

Acquire knowledge. It enables the possessers to distinguish the right from the wrong; it lightens up the path to Heaven. It is a friend in the desert, our company in solitude, our companion when friendless.

It guides to happiness, it sustains in adversity. It is an ornament among friends and an armour against enemies. *–Koran*

✱

EGOISM

None is so empty as those who are full of themselves.

–Benjamin Whichcotte

✱

A man who is in love with himself will have no rivals.

–Benjamin Franklin

✱

ELOQUENCE

True eloquence consists in saying all that is necessary and nothing but what is necessary.

–La Rochefoucauld

✱

Eloquence is the poetry of prose. *–Bryant*

✱

Eloquence may exist without a proportional degree of wisdom. *–Edmond Burke*

✱

ENEMY AND FRIEND

He that wrestles with us strengthens our nerves and sharpens our skill. Our antagonist is our helper.

–Edmond Burke

✱

The wise man learns more from his enemies than the fool from his friends. *–Jacques Deval*

✳

One should lift oneself by one's own efforts and should not degrade oneself; for one's own self is one's friend and one's self is one's enemy.

To him who has subdued the lower self by the higher self, the self acts like a friend. Even so the very self of him who has not conquered his lower self behaves antagonistically like an enemy. *–Bhagavat Gita*

✳

ENTHUSIASM

Enthusiasm leads to success. Enthusiasm is happiness. Enthusiasm is always the driving force to all actions. *–The Ramayana*

✳

Nothing great was ever achieved without enthusiasm. *–Emerson*

✳

The prudent man may direct a state; but it is the enthusiast who regenerates it, or ruins it. *–Lord Lytton*

✳

National enthusiasm is the great nursery of genius. *–H.T. Tuckerman*

✳

ENVY

Envy is ignorance; imitation is suicide. *–Anon*

✳

Envy and fear are the only passions to which no pleasure is attached. *–Collins*

✳

Envy is a kind of praise. *–Gray*

✳

It is better to be envied than pitied. *–Herodotus*

✳

ERROR

To err is human, to forgive is divine. *–Pope*

✳

The cautious seldom err. *–Conculus*

✳

One of the most dangerous forms of human error is forgetting what one is trying to achieve.

–Paul Nitze

✳

A man can make mistakes, but only an idiot persists in his error. *–Cicero*

✳

No man should be judged by his defects. The great virtues a man has are his; but his errors are the common weaknesses of humanity and should never be counted in estimating his character.

–Swami Vivekananda

✳

ESTIMATE

Do not underestimate a child or overestimate a grown-up. *–Akbarali Jetha*

✳

EVIL

Resist not evil by doing evil in return, but make a show of resistance with a view to defending oneself. *–Sri Ramakrishna*

✳

Evil allures, but good endures. *–Leo Tolstoy*

✳

The evil that men do lives after them. *–Shakespeare*

✳

For every evil under the sun,
There is a remedy, or there is none;
If there be one, try and find it,
If there be none, never mind it. *–Hazlitt*

✳

All that is necessary for the triumph of evil is that good men do nothing. *–Edmund Burke*

✳

EXAMPLE

Example is always more efficacious than precept. *–Dr. Johnson*

✳

The most valuable gift you can give another is a good example. *–Anon*

✳

Lives of great men all remind us we can make our lives sublime. And, departig, leave behind us foot prints on the sands of time. *–Longfellow*

*

Children have more need of models than of critics. *–Joubert*

*

EXPECTATION

The surest way to puncture a pleasure is to over-anticipate it; the best things in life are not free, but unexpected. *–Sydney Harris*

*

EXPERIENCE

Experience is the child of thought, and thought is the child of action. *–Disraeli*

*

Experience keeps a dear school, yet fools will learn in no other. *–Benjamin Franklin*

*

Big things, in themselves, are only a multiplication in intensified form of a myriad of accomplished little things. Everything you have ever mastered in life remains to serve you. Everything you have not mastered remains to hamper you. *–Harold Sherman*

*

Experience convinces me that permanent good can never be the outcome of untruth and violence.

–Mahatma Gandhi

✵

Experience is a wonderful thing; it enables you to recognize a mistake every time you repeat it. *–A.P.*

✵

Experience is not what happens to a man; it is what a man does with what happens to him.

–Aldous Huxley

✵

Experience is the best of school masters, only the school fees are heavy. *–Carlyle*

✵

FAILURE

Real failure comes only when we forget our ideals, objectives and principles and begin to wander away from the road which leads to their realization.

–Jawaharlal Nehru

✵

Failures are the stepping stones of success.

–Popular Saying

✵

You may be disappointed if you fail, but you are doomed if you do not try. *–Beverly Hills*

✵

There is pathos in the sight of a man who, having tried, has failed-but infinitely greater sadness is there in the contemplation of him who will not try because he is indifferent. *–Henry S. Merriman*

*

Our greatest glory is not never falling, but in rising every time we fall. *–Oliver Goldsmith*

*

In the lexicon of youth, which fate reserves for a bright manhood, there is no such word as fail!

–Bulwer Lytton

*

Not failure, but low aim, is crime. *–Browning*

*

FAITH

In actual life, every great enterprise begins with and takes its first step in faith. *–August W. Schlegal*

*

Who has faith, has all, and he who lacks faith lacks all. It is faith in the name of the Lord that works wonders, for faith is life and doubt is death.

–Sri Ramakrishna

*

Faith only begins where reason falters.

–Mahatma Gandhi

*

FAME

Fame is the perfume of heroic deeds. *–Socrates*

✳

If a man can write a better book, preach a better sermon, or make a better mouse-trap, than his neighbour, though he builds his house in the woods, the world will make a beaten path to his door.

–Emerson

✳

What a heavy burden is a name that has become too famous. *–Voltaire*

✳

Fame is the thirst of youth. *–Byron*

✳

FATE

Fate bows to the man who defies it.

–Swami Ramtirth

✳

Let us, then, be up and doing, with a heart for any fate. *–Longfellow*

✳

We make our fortunes and we call them fate.

–Disraeli

✳

FAULT

They say best men are moulded out of faults;
And for the most, become much more
the better for being a little bad! *–Shakespeare*

✳

The greatest of faults, I should say, is to be conscious of none. *–Carlyle*

*

A fault confessed is half redressed. *–H.G. Bohn*

*

FEAR

There is a time to take counsel of your fears, and there is a time to never listen to any fear.

–Gen. George Patton

*

The only thing we have to fear is fear itself.

–F.D. Roosevelt

*

Fear always springs from ignorance. *–Emerson*

*

Let us fear God, and we shall cease to fear man.

–Mahatma Gandhi

*

In enjoyment, there is the fear of disease; in social position, the fear of falling off; in wealth, the fear of thieves; in honour, the fear of humiliation; in power, the fear of foes; in beauty, the fear of old age; in erudition, the fear of opponents; in virtue the fear of traducers; in body, the fear of death. For men all things of this world are attended with fear. Renuciation alone assures fearlessness.

–Bharthruhari

*

FIRST IMPRESSION

You never get a second chance to make a good first impression!

–Anon

*

FLATTERY

It is easy to flatter; it is harder to praise.

–Jean Paul Richter

*

Flattery is counterfeit money which, but for vanity, would have no circulation.

–La Rouchefaucauld

*

Flattery corrupts both the receiver and the giver.

–Burke

*

FLOWER

The first flower that blossomed on this earth was an invitation to the unborn song.

–Rabindranath Tagore

*

I cannot see what flowers are at my feet. *–Keats*

*

Flowers are words which even a babe may understand.

–Aurthur C. Coxe

*

Full many a flower is born to blush unseen,
And wastes its sweetness on the desert air. *–Gray*

*

FOOLS

I assure you that a learned fool is more foolish than an ignorant fool. *–Moliere*

✷

Fools rush in where angels fear to tread. *–Pope*

✷

What fools these mortals be! *–Shakespeare*

✷

Let a fool be made serviceable according to his folly. *–Joseph Conrad*

✷

A fool and his money are soon parted. *–Proverb*

✷

Love is the wisdom of the fool and the folly of the wise. *–Dr. Johnson*

✷

FORCE

What is readily yielded to courtesy is never yielded to force. *–Mahatma Gandhi*

✷

Brute force bends; fair argument convinces. *–Vergilla Zoppi*

✷

Force is all-conquering, but its victories are short-lived. *–Abraham Lincoln*

✷

The power that is supported by force alone, will have cause often to tremble. *–Kossuth*

✳

FORETHOUGHT

To be forewarned is to be forearmed. *–Cervantes*

✳

In life, as in chess, forethought wins.

–Charles Buxton

✳

Foresight is more important than forethought.

–Napoleon

✳

FORGIVENESS

Abstinence is forgiveness only when there is power to punish. It is meaningless when it proceeds from a helpless creature. *–Mahatma Gandhi*

✳

Forgiveness adorns a soldier. *–Mahatma Gandhi*

✳

Write injuries in dust, benefits in marble.

–Benjamin Franklin

✳

FORTUNE

Fortune gives too much to many, enough to nobody. *–Martial*

✳

Fortune favours the brave. *–Proverb*

*

Every man is the architect of his own fortune. *–Sallust*

*

Fortune and love befriend the bold. *–Ovid*

*

There is a tide in the affairs of men, which taken at the flood, leads on to fortune. *–Shakespeare*

*

FREEDOM

Freedom is not worth having if it does not connote freedom to err. *–Mahatma Gandhi*

*

A man who is made for freedom has got to take tremendous risks and stake everything. *–Mahatma Gandhi*

*

We gain freedom when we have paid the price for our right to live. *–Rabindranath Tagore*

*

Every freedom in this world is limited; limited not so much by law as by circumstances. *–Jawaharlal Nehru*

*

Political freedom which we have won at much cost and sacrifice, is only an opportunity. It is not a fulfilment. *–Dr. S. Radhakrishnan*

✷

Liberty has restraints, but no frontiers.

–Lloyd George

✷

Freedom is my birth right and I shall have it.

–Lokmanya Tilak

✷

Freedom is nothing else but a chance to be better.

–Albert Camus

✷

Liberty will not descend to people: people must raise themselves to it; it is a blessing that must be earned before it can be enjoyed. *–Colton*

✷

FRIENDSHIP

Oh! the comfort, the inexpressible comfort of feeling safe with a person having neither to weigh thought nor measure words, but to pour them all just as they are-chaff and grain together, knowing that a faithful hand will take and sift them, keep what is worth and then, with the breadth of kindness, blow the rest away.

–Anon

✷

If you want an accounting of your worth, count your friends. *–Merry Browne*

✳

In prosperity, our friends know us,
In adversity, we know our friends. *–John C. Collius*

✳

Friends are like antiques. The longer you have them, the more valuable they become. *–Anon*

✳

The only way to have a true friend is to be a true friend. *–Emerson*

✳

Those friends thou hast and their adoption tried, grapple them to thy soul with hoops of steel.

–Shakespeare

✳

A friendship which exacts oneness of opinion and conduct, is not worth much. *–Mahatma Gandhi*

✳

FUTURE

Take care of the present and the future will take care of itself. *–English Proverb*

✳

When all else is lost, the future still remains.

–Bovee

✳

I believe the future is only the past, again entered through another gate. *–Pinero*

✳

GENIUS

Genius means a transcendent capacity for taking trouble. *–Carlyle*

⁕

Doing easily what others find difficult is talent, doing what is impossible for talent is genius. *–Amiel*

⁕

Genius is one per cent inspiration and ninety-nine per cent perspiration *–Thomas A. Edison*

⁕

Genius is only an infinite capacity for taking pains. *–Jane E. Hopkins*

⁕

GENTLEMAN

A gentleman is a man who is never rude unintentionally. *–Machael Arlen*

⁕

A gentleman is a man who can disagree without being disagreeable. *–Anon*

⁕

A TRUE GENTLEMAN

The true gentleman carefully avoids whatever may cause a jar or a jolt in the minds of those with whom he is cast; all clashing of opinion, or collision of feeling, all restraint, or suspicion, or gloom, or resentment, his great concern being to make every one at their ease and at home. He is tender towards the bashful, gentle towards the distant, and merciful towards the absurd.

He guards against unseasonable allusions, or topics which may irritate. He makes light of favours, and seems to be receiving when he is conferring. He has no ears for slander or gossip. He is never mean or little in his disputes, never takes unfair advantage.

From a long sighted prudence he observes the maxim that we should ever conduct ourselves towards our enemy as if he is one day to be our firend.

He is patient, forbearing and resigned. He submits to pain because it is inevitable, and to death, because it is his destiny. *–Cardinal Newman*

⁕

GLORY

Glory lies in the attempt to reach one's goal and not in reaching it. *–Mahatma Gandhi*

⁕

Sound, sound the clarion, fill the fife,
To all the sensual world proclaim
One crowded hour of glorious life
Is worth an age without a name. *–Walter Scott*

⁕

GOD

God is Truth. *–Mahatma Gandhi*

*

If I make the seven oceans ink, if I make the trees my pen, if I make the earth my paper, the glory of God cannot be written. *–Kabir*

*

Those who would be children of God, must take good heed that their words be simple, clear, truthful and guileless. *–St. Francis of Sales*

*

No man can serve two masters; for either he will hate the one and love the other; or else he will hold to one and despise the other. You cannot serve God and mammon. *–Mathew*

*

Glorious indeed is the world of God around us; but more glorious, the world of God within us.

–Longfellow

*

To God belongeth the East and the West; therefore, whither soever you turn to pray, there is the word of God, for God is omnipresent and omniscient.

–Koran

God is not a cosmic bell-boy for whom we can press a button to get things. *–Harry E. Fosdick*

*

GOODNESS

He that does good to another, does good also to himself, not only in the consequences, but in the very act; for the consciousness of well-doing is, in itself, ample reward. *–Seneca*

*

The good shine from afar like the Himalayan range, while those lacking virtue, vanish unseen, as arrows shot in dark night. *–Gautama Buddha*

*

He who is too busy doing good, finds no time to be good. *–Rabindranath Tagore*

*

There is nothing either good or bad but thinking makes it so. *–Shakespeare*

*

GRACE

Men would obtain great favours from God did they expend half the pains on acquiring His grace that they do on procuring the favour of the world.

–St. Thomas Acquinas

*

GRATITUDE

Gratitude is the memory of the heart. *–J.B. Massien*

✷

Gatitude is a fruit of great cultivation. You do not find it among gross people. *–Samuel Johnson*

✷

Gatitude is a duty which ought to be paid, but which none a right to expect. *–Rosseau*

✷

GREATNESS

Be not afraid of greatness. Some are born great; some achieve greatness and some have greatness thrust upon them. *–Shakespeare*

✷

No great man lives in vain. The history of the world is but the biography of great men. *–Carlyle*

✷

The greatest truths are the simplest, and so are the greatest men. *–A.W. Hare*

✷

We cannot all be great, but we can attach ourselves to something that is great. *–Harry E. Fosdick*

✷

The heights by great men reached and kept,
Were not attained by sudden flight,
But they, while their companions slept,
Were toiling upward in the night. *–Longfellow*

✷

Lives of great men all remind us,
We can make our lives sublime.
And, departing, leave behind us,
Footprints in the sands of time. *–Longfellow*

✳

Great minds have purposes, others have wishes.

–Washington Irving

✳

Greatness comes from vision, the tolerance of the spirit, compassion and an even temper which is not ruffled by ill fortune or good fortune.

–Jawaharlal Nehru

✳

Whatever a great man does, that very thing other men also do; whatever standard he sets up the generality of men follow the same. *–Bhagavat Gita*

✳

HABITS

The chains of habits are generally too small to be felt until they are too strong to be broken.

–Dr. Johnson

✳

Sow an act, and you reap a habit. Sow a habit, and you reap a character. Sow a character and you reap a destiny. *–Charles Reade*

✳

How use doth breed a habit in a man. *–Shakespeare*

✳

Habit: the shackles of the free. *–Ambrose Bierce*

✳

HANDS

A hand to touch me in the dark room, breaking the long loneliness. *–Carl Sandburg*

✳

The hand that rocks the cradle is the hand that rules the world. *–William R. Wallace*

✳

The loving touch of the hand, the gentle and winsome tone that you had no time or thought for with trouble enough of your own. *–Margaret E. Sanger*

✳

HAPPINESS

It is one of the paradoxes of psychology that the pursuit of happiness defeats its own purpose. We find happiness only when we do not directly seek it.

–J. Arthur Hadfield

✳

Happiness and work are really wedded together, for there can be no true happiness without the feeling that one is doing something worthwhile.

–Jawaharlal Nehru

✳

Happiness is where it is found, and seldom where it is sought. *–Josh Billings*

*

There is no happiness in anything we do unless it is the beneficiary of the stamp of approval of the society we live in. *–Friedrich Nietzche*

*

The best kind of feeling good (happiness) is feeling good for no special reason. This kind lasts the longest.

–Theodore Ruben

*

Is it your desire to live long and happy? Then keep your tongue from evil, keep your lips from deceit. Shun evil and do good, seek to be friendly—aim at that. *–Psalms*

*

Everyone carries in himself the sources of his own happiness or wretchedness. Circumstances have really very little to do with our inner experience. It is self, after all that in largest measure gives the colour to our skies and the tone to the music we hear.

–J.R. Miller, D.D.

*

There is this difference between happiness and wisdom; he that thinks himself the happiest man is really so; but he that thinks himself the wisest man is generally the greatest fool. *–Colton*

The most happy is he who most promotes the happiness of others. *–Zarathushtra*

✳

A few more smiles of silent sympathy, a few more tender words, a little more restraint on temper—they make all the difference between happiness and half happiness to those with whom we live. *–Anon*

✳

The tragedy of human history is decreasing happiness in the midst of increasing comfort.

–Swami Chinmayananda

✳

Happiness consists in activity. It is a running stream and not a stagnant pool. *–J.M. Good*

✳

Happiness is a perfume you cannot pour on others without getting a few drops on yourself. *–Anon*

✳

Happiness is the only good, the place to be happy is here, the time to be happy is now, the way to be happy is to make others so. *–Robert Ingersoll*

✳

You have no more right to consume happiness without producing it than to consume wealth without producing it. *–George Bernard Shaw*

✳

HATE

Hate is the subtlest form of violence.

–Mahatma Gandhi

✳

Never in this world can hatred be stilled by hatred. It will only be stilled by non-hatred. This is the law eternal. *–Gautama Buddha*

✳

There are many roads to hatred, but envy is one of the shortest of them all. *–Lignorium*

✳

Hating people is like burning down your own house to get rid of a rat. *–Harry E. Fosdick*

✳

We have just enough religion to make us hate, but not enough to make us love one another. *–Swift*

✳

HEALTH

Health is really a by-product of a normally active, busy, clean and interested life. And you will notice that our health is always better when we don't need to think about it at all; in other words, when it is the natural bloom of an orderly life. *–James Black*

✳

There is no curing a sick man who believes himself in health. *–Amiel*

✳

Health is not a condition of matter, but of mind, nor can the material senses bear reliable testimony on the subject of health. *–Mary Baker Eddy*

✳

The preservation of health is a duty. Few seem conscious that there is such a thing as physical morality. *–Herbert Spencer*

✳

HEART

There is dew in one flower and not in another, because one opens its cup and takes it in, while the other closes itself and the drops run off.

So God rains goodness and mercy as wide as the dew, and if we lack them, it is because we do not open our hearts to receive them. *–Aughey*

✳

It is difficult to smile with an aching heart. *–Anon*

✳

The heart of the fool is in his mouth, but the mouth of the wise man is in his heart. *–Benjamin Franklin*

✳

Where your treasure is, there your heart be also.

–Bible

✳

HEAVEN

Heaven means to be one with God. *–Confucius*

✳

Heaven and hell are not physical areas. A soul tormented with remorse for its deeds is hell; a soul with satisfaction of life well lived is heaven. The reward of virtuous living is the good life itself.

–Dr. S. Radhakrishnan

*

The mind is its own place, and in itself can make a Heaven of hell, a hell of Heaven. *–Milton*

*

I never spoke with God, nor visited in Heaven; yet certain am I of the spot as if the chart were given.

–Emily Dickinson

*

HELP

It is one of the most beautiful compensations of life that no man helps another without helping himself.

–Anon

*

When you are good to others, you are best to yourself.

–Dale Carnegie

*

I am going your way, so let us go hand in hand. You help me and I will help you. Let us help one another while we may. *–William Morris*

*

Bounty always receives a part of its value from the manner in which it is bestowed. *–Dr. Johnson*

✳

What do we live for if it is not to make life less difficult for each other? *–George Eliot*

✳

This body is meant for helping others. *–Kalidasa*

✳

You can get anything in this world you want if you help people get what they want. *–Anon*

✳

HISTORY

The events of history reflect the events in the soul of men. *–Dr. S. Radhakrishnan*

✳

In a true sense, history is a struggle of man to reach beyond himself, to approximate to the ideal of freedom and human concord. *–Dr. S. Radhakrishnan*

✳

Men of law lay down constitutions, but history is really made by great minds, large hearts and stout arms. *–Jawaharlal Nehru*

✳

Man does not reveal himself in his history, he struggles up through it. *–Rabindranath Tagore*

✳

HOME

Every home is a university and parents are the teachers. *–Mahatma Gandhi*

✳

Home is where the heart is. *–Pliny*

✳

Charity begins at home. *–Thomas Browne*

✳

Keep the home fires burning; while your hearts are yearning. Though your lads are far away they dream of home. *–Lena A. Ford*

✳

HONESTY

An honest man is the noblest work of God. *–Pope*

✳

Honesty is the best policy. *–English Proverb*

✳

No legacy is so rich as honesty. *–Shakespeare*

✳

Honesty once pawned is never redeemed.

–Thomas Middleton

✳

HOPE

It is necessary to hope, for hope itself is happiness; whatever enlarges hope will exalt courage. The natural flights of the human mind are not from pleasure to pleasure, but from hope to hope.

–Dr. Johnson

*

Hope springs eternal in the human breast; man never is, but always to be blest. *–Pope*

*

Hope for the best, and be prepared for the worst.

–English Proverb

*

HUMANITY

After all there is but one race—humanity.

–George Moore

*

Our true nationality is mankind. *–H.G. Wells*

*

Everybody thinks of changing humanity but nobody thinks of changing oneself. *–Leo Tolstoy*

*

You must not lose faith in humanity. Humanity is an ocean; if a few drops of the ocean are dirty, the ocean itself does not become dirty. *–Daniel Schorr*

*

HUMILITY

A fault which humbles a man is of more use to him than a good action which puffs him up.

–Thomas Wilson

*

Fruit-laden trees bend down to earth. The water-laden clouds hang low; good men are not puffed up by power. The unselfish are by nature humble.

–Kalidasa

❋

The tree laden with fruits always bends low. If you wish to be great, be lowly and meek.

–Sri Ramakrishna

❋

I believe the first test of a truly great man is his humility. *–Ruskin*

❋

HUNGER

Poor men eat more excellent food than the rich, for hunger gives it sweetness. *–Mahabharata*

❋

No man can be a patriot on an empty stomach.

–W.C. Brann

❋

An empty stomach is not a good political adviser.

–Albert Einstein

❋

THE HUMAN TOUCH

'Tis the human touch in this world that counts, the touch of your hand and mine, which means far more to the failing heart than shelter and bread and wine; The shelter is gone when the night is o'er, and bread lasts only a day. But the touch of the hand and the sound of the voice sing on in the soul always.

–Spencer M. Free

✳

The touch of human hands-
That is the boon we ask;
For groping, day by day,
Along the stony way,
We need the comrade heart
That understands,
And the warmth, the living warmth of human hands.
The touch of human hands;
Not vain, unthinking words,
Not that cold charity
Which shuns our misery:
We seek a loyal friend
Who understands,
And the warmth, the pulsating warmth of human hands...

–Thomas Curtis Clark

✳

IDEA

Nothing is more dangerous than idea when it is the only one we have. *–Emile Chartier*

✳

Ideas are nobody's property; they belong to whoever expresses them best. *–Emilio Cecchi*

✳

How wonderful it would be to take every worn-out idea and throw it out at midnight on New Year's Eve! What a relief to get rid of every old resentment! What healthy-mindedness would result if we were to take every old fear that has been held for so long and dispose of it. How great it would be to get rid of old prejudices, old notions, old ways of doing things!

–Norman Vincent Peale

✳

IDEALS AND IDEALIST

Doing good is very good, but that comes from thinking... Fill the brain, therefore, with high thoughts, highest ideals, place them day and night before you and out of it will come great work.

–Swami Vivekananda

An invasion of armies can be resisted, but not an idea whose time has come. *–Victor Hugo*

Our ideals are our better selves. *–A.B. Alcott*

We have to function in line with the highest ideals of the age we live in, though we may add to them or seek to mould them in accordance with our national genius. Those ideals may be classified under two heads: humanism and the scientific spirit.

–Jawaharlal Nehru

Ideals are like stars; You will not succeed in touching them with your hands. But like the sea-faring man on the desert of waters, you choose them as your guides, and following them, you will reach your destiny. *–Charles Schurz*

*

Ah, but man's reach should exceed his grasp. Or what's heaven for? *–Browning*

*

IDLENESS

The man who is always killing time is killing his own chances in life. The man destined for success, makes time live by making every minute useful.

–Arthur Brisbane

*

Difficulty is, for the most part, the daughter of idleness. *–Dr. Johnson*

*

The idle man's brain is the devil's workshop.

–English Proverb

*

It were better to live one single day in the commencement of strong endeavour than to live a hundred years of idleness and lassitude.

–Gautama Buddha

*

IGNORANCE

Ignorance is the night of the mind but a night without moon or star. *–Confucius*

✻

Where ignorance is bliss it is folly to be wise.

–T. Gray

✻

Ignorance never settles a question. *–Disracli*

✻

Ignorance of the law excuses no man. *–John Selden*

✻

ILL DEEDS

How often the sight of means to do ill deeds make ill deeds done. *–Shakespeare*

✻

IMAGINATION

Imagination is as good as many voyages and how much cheaper! *–George W. Curtis*

✻

He who has imagination without learning has wings but no feet. *–Joseph Joubert*

✻

There are lots of people who mistake their imagination for their memory. *–John Billings*

✻

It is imagination which rules the human race.

–Napoleon

✳

Imagination is useful only as long as it remains practical. *–Alexis R. Wren*

✳

IMITATION

Almost all absurdity of conduct arises from the imitation of those whom we cannot resemble.

–Dr. Johnson

✳

Imitation is the sincerest form of flattery. *–Colton*

✳

Imitation is suicide. *–Emerson*

✳

No man was ever great by imitation. *–Dr. Johnson*

✳

IMPATIENCE

Impatience can be virtue if you practise it on yourself.

–Rod Mekuen

✳

IMPOSSIBLE

Impossibility is a word only to be found in the dictionary of fools. *–Napoleon*

✳

Few things are impossible to diligence and skill.

–Dr. Johnson

✳

INDIVIDUAL

An institution is the lengthened shadow of one man.

–Emerson

Every individual has a place to fill in the world, and is important in some respect, whether he chooses to be so or not. *–Hawthorne*

✳

The worth of a state, in the long run, is the worth of the individuals composing it. *–John Stewart Mill*

INEVITABLE

Co-operate with the inevitable. *–Dale Carnegic*

"It is so, it cannot be otherwise".

–Inscription on a Cathedral Wall

Be willing to have it so. Acceptance of what has happened is the first step to overcoming the consequences of any misfortune. *–William James*

For every ailment under the sun, there is a remedy or there is none. If there be one, try to find it. If there be none, never mind it. *–An Old Rhyme*

God, grant me the serenity, to accept the things I cannot change. The courage to change the things I can. And the wisdom to know the difference.

–Dr. Reinhold Niebuhr

✳

INFLUENCE

The value of every life depends on its influence on other lives. *–Herbert Casson*

✳

The humblest individual exerts some influence, either for good or evil, upon others. *–Henry Ward Beecher*

✳

INJURY

As all have to sleep together laid low on the earth, why do the foolish wish to injure one another?

–Mahabharata

✳

An injury is much sooner forgotten than an insult.

–Lord Chesterfield

✳

Recompense injury with justice, and recompense kindness with kindness. *–Confucius*

✳

INTOLERANCE

Intolerance betrays want of faith in one's cause.

–Mahatma Gandhi

✳

INVESTMENT

Some people treat life like a slot machine, trying to put in as little as possible and hoping to hit a jackpot; wiser people think life as a solid investment from which they receive in terms of what they have put in.

–Anon

✳

If a man empties his purse into his head, no man can take it away from him. An investment in knowledge always pays the best interest. *–Benjamin Franklin*

✳

JOY

Joy is in the battle. The result comes by the grace of God. *–Mahatma Gandhi*

✳

I wish you all the joy that you can wish.

–Shakespeare

✳

Great joys, like grief, are silent. *–S. Marmion*

✳

JUDGEMENT

In judging others, a man labours to no purpose, commonly errs and easily sins, but in examining and judging himself, he is always wisely and usefully employed. *–Thomas A. Kempis*

✳

Judge not, lest ye be judged. *–Bible*

✳

Four things belong to a judge; to hear courteously, to answer wisely, to consider soberly and to decide impartially. *–Socrates*

✳

JUSTICE

If you should bend the staff of justice, do not bend it under the weight of money, but under that of mercy. *–Cervantes*

✳

Live and let live is the rule of common justice. *–Sir Roger L' Estrange*

✳

Justice is truth in action. *–Disraeli*

✳

There is no virtue so truly great and God-like as justice. *–Addison*

✳

KIND, KINDNESS

Kindness is the foundation of all religions; pride, the parent of all sins. *–Sant Tulsidas*

✳

A part of kindness consists in loving people more than they deserve. *–J. Joubert*

✳

Kindness gives birth to kindness. *–Sophocles*

✳

Men are cruel, but man is kind.

–Rabindranath Tagore

✳

Little deeds of kindness, little words of love, help to make earth happy like the heaven above.

–Julia A.F. Carney

✳

Have you had a kindness shown, pass it on; it was not given for thee alone, pass it on; let it travel down the years. Let it wipe another's tears. Till in Heaven the deed appears—pass it on. *–Henry Burton*

✳

I expect to pass through this world but once; any good thing therefore that I can do, or any kindness that I can show to any fellow creature, let me do it and now; let me not defer or neglect it, for I shall not pass this way again. *–Stephen Grellet*

✳

KNOWLEDGE

Knowledge is power *–Hobbes*

✳

Knowledge is the only instrument of production that is not subject to diminishing returns. *–J.M. Clark*

✳

That knowledge which purifies the mind and heart alone is true knowledge; all else is only a negation of knowledge. *–Sri Ramakrishna*

✳

The law of nature is that a certain quantity of work is necessary to product a certain quantity of good of any kind, whatever.

If you want knowledge, you must toil for it.

–John Ruskin

✳

We broaden our field of knowledge and reach generalisations of considerable magnitude as the result of numerous small thoughts brought together in the mind and carefully considered.

–Alexander G. Bell

✳

Knowledge is of two kinds. We know one subject ourselves or we know where we can get information upon it. *–Dr. Johnson*

✳

Knowledge comes, but wisdom lingers. *–Tennyson*

✳

Science is organised knowledge. *–Herbert Spencer*

✳

Knowledge is proud that he has learned, wisdom is humble that he knows no more. *–Cowper*

✳

All information is not knowledge; all knowledge is not wisdom. *–Anon*

✳

LAUGHTER

Laugh and the world laughs with you, weep and you weep alone. *–Ella W. Wilcox*

✳

There is health and goodness in the mirth.
In which an honest laugh has birth. *–Anon*

✳

It is more fitting for a man to laugh at life than to lament over it. *–Seneca*

✳

The art of medicine consists of amusing the patient while nature cures the disease. *–Voltaire*

✳

Humour is a whisper from the soul, imploring mind and body to relax, let go and be at peace again.

–Anon

✳

Care to our coffin adds a nail, no doubt; and every laugh, so merry, draws one out. *–Wolcolt*

✳

Humour is an affirmation of dignity, a declaration of man's superiority to all that befalls him.

–Romain Gary

✳

Good humour is one of the best articles of dress one can wear in society. *–W. M. Thackeray*

✳

A laugh is worth a thousand groans in any market.

–Charles Lamb

*

I am persuaded that every time a man smiles, but much more when he laughs, it adds something to this fragment of life. *–Lawrence Sterne*

*

It has always seemed to me that a hearty laughter is a good way to jog internally without having to go outdoors. *–Norman Cousins*

*

LEADER

A good team leader is someone who takes a little more than his share of the blame and a little less of his share of the credit. *–Anon*

*

LEARNING

We are not born with the secret of how to live. There are things we must learn. *–Mildred Newman*

*

Remember that there is something to be learned from every body. Each of us has a story to tell and a unique perspective. The way to try to understand the world is to see it from as many different view-points as possible. *–Ari Kiev, M.D.*

*

Wear your learning like your watch in a private pocket; and do not pull it out and strike, merely to show that you have one. *(Compiler: In olden days people had only pocket watches, wrist watch is a later development).* *–Chesterfield*

✳

Learning without thinking is useless. Thinking without learning is dangerous. *–Confucius*

✳

LIFE

To enjoy life one should give up the lure of life.

–Mahatma Gandhi

✳

One crowded hour of glorious life is worth an age without a name. *–Walter Scott*

✳

Our body is like the foam of the sea, our life like a bird, our company with those whom we love does not last for ever; why then, weepest thou, my son?

–Mahabharata

✳

Life must always be a great adventure. With risks on every hand, a clear–sighted eye, a many sided sympathy, a fine daring, an endless patience, are ever necessary to all good living. *–Havelock Ellis*

✳

Life consists not in holding good cards but in playing those you do, well. *–Josh Billings*

✳

Life will always be, to a great extent, what we ourselves make it. The cheerful man makes a cheerful world, the gloomy man, a gloomy one. We usually find but our own temperament reflected in the disposition of those about us. If we are ourselves querulous, we will find them so; if we were unforgiving and uncharitable to them, they will be the same to us. *–Anon*

✳

I find life an exciting business—and most exciting when it is lived for others. *–Helen Keller*

✳

Great things can be done by great sacrifice only.
–Swami Vivekananda

✳

It is a funny thing about life if you refuse to accept anything but the best, you will get it!
–Somerset Maugham

✳

LITTLE THINGS

There are no little things with God *–Anon*

✳

Trifles make perfection and perfection is no trifle.
–Michael Angelo

✳

LIVING

Live so that your friends can defend you but never have to. *–Arnold Glason*

✳

Living is the art of getting used to what we did not expect. *–Eleanor Wood*

✳

Do all the good you can. In all the ways you can. In all the places you can. At all the times you can. To all the people you can. As long as you ever can. *–Ingersoll*

✳

We live in deeds, not years. *–Longfellow*

✳

Live well today, and every yesterday will become a dream of happiness, and every tomorrow will be a vision of hope. *–Sanskrit Verse*

✳

LOGIC

Logic is sword, all blades and no handle. It bleeds the hand that holds it. *–Rabindranath Tagore*

✳

LOOKING FORWARD

Looking forward to something you deeply desire is one of the most satisfying of all experiences. Those who are deprived of it are deprived indeed. *–Judson Gooding*

✳

It is a mistake to look too far ahead. Only one link in the chain of destiny can be handled at a time.

–Winston Churchill

✳

LOSS

You are never a loser until you quit trying.

–Mike Ditka

✳

The cheerful loser is a winner. *–Elbert Hubbard*

✳

Wise men never sit and wail their loss, but cheerly seek how to redress their harms. *–Shakespeare*

✳

LOVE

He is the true man who loves God, loves man and, serving all, abides in eternal love. *–Guru Nanak*

✳

I am able to love my God because he gives me freedom to deny him. *–Rabindranath Tagore*

✳

God is love, love is God. *–Kabir*

✳

The love the world most needs today, is the love that restores unity and resists division, that turns sacrifice into offering, changes obstacles into opportunities and subordinates self while it elevates service.

–W.R.R.

✳

Man is not made for hate and destruction but for love and life. *–Dr. S. Radhakrishnan*

✳

Love sought is good, but given unsought is better.

–Shakespeare

✳

Love conquers all; let us too yield to love. *–Virgil*

✳

Love is not love which alters when its alteration finds.

–Shakespeare

✳

Pure knowledge and pure love are one and the same. Both lead the aspirants to God. The path of love is much easier. *–Sri Ramakrishna*

✳

Greater love hath no man than this, that a man lay down his life for another. *–Bible*

✳

LUCK

Shallow men believe in luck. Strong men believe in cause and effect. *–Emerson*

✳

True luck consists not in holding the best of cards at the table: luckiest is he who knows just when to rise and go home! *–John Hay*

✳

Luck never gives; it only lends. *–Swedish Proverb*

✳

MAN

Men, men, these are wanted; everything else will be ready, but strong, vigorous, believing young men, sincere to the backbone are wanted. A hundred such and the world becomes revolutionised.

–Swami Vivekananda

✳

One machine can do the work of fifty ordinary men. No machine can do the work of one extraordinary man! *–Elbert Hubbard*

✳

Seekest thou God? Then see him in man; His Divinity is manifest more in man than in any other object. Man is the greatest manifestation of God.

–Sri Ramakrishna

✳

God created man in his own image. *–Bible*

✳

Taste is the mark of an educated man, imagination the sign of a productive man, an emotional balance the token of a mature man. *–Emerson*

✳

It is easy to find men who always talk of pleasing things. But men who talk of things that are beneficial though not pleasing to the ear, are rare indeed.

–Ramayana

✳

MANNERS

The test of good manners is being able to put up pleasantly with bad ones. *–Anon*

✳

Good breeding consists in concealing how much we think of ourselves and how little we think of the other fellow. *–Mark Twain*

✳

Manners must adorn knowledge and smoothen its way through the world. *–Chesterfield*

✳

MEMORIES

The best things you can give children, next to good habits, are good memories. *–Sydney Harris*

✳

Better by far you should forget and smile, than that you should remember and be sad.

–Christina Rossetti

✳

God gave us memories so that we might have roses in December. *–J.M. Barrie*

✳

MERRIMENT

He that is of a merry heart hath a continual feast.

–The Book of Proverbs.

✳

A merry heart maketh a cheerful countenance.

–Old Testament

✳

The best doctors in the world are Doctor Diet, Doctor Quiet and Doctor Merryman. *–Swift*

✳

MIND

Great minds have purposes, others have wishes. Little minds are tamed and subdued by misfortune, but great minds rise above them. *–Washington Inving*

✳

A sound mind in a sound body *–Juvenal*

✳

What is mind? No matter. What is matter? Never mind! *–T.H. Key*

✳

The mind is its own place, and in itself can make a heaven of hell, a hell of heaven. *–Milton*

✳

A man's mind is steady when he withdraws his senses from sense objects as the tortoise its limbs from all sides. *–Bhagavat Gita*

✳

Neither father nor mother nor kindred can confer greater benefits than does the well-directed mind.

–Gautama Buddha

✳

MISERY

The secret of being miserable is to have the leisure to bother about whether you are happy or not.

–Bernard Shaw

✳

Fire tries gold, misery tries brave men. *–Seneca*

✳

Resolve to be thyself and know that he who finds himself loses his misery. *–Mathew Arnold*

✳

MISFORTUNE

Behind every big disaster are many little mistakes.

–Miguel A. Tapia

✳

There is, properly speaking, no misfortune in the world. Happiness and misfortune stand in a continual balance. Every misfortune is, as it were, the obstruction of a stream which, after overcoming this obstacle, but bursts through with greater force.

–Novalis

✳

Misfortunes always come in by a door that has been left open for them. *–Proverb*

✳

The wise man sees in the misfortunes of others what he should avoid. *–Syrus*

✳

MOTHER

Mother is the name of God in the lips and hearts of little children. *–Thackeray*

✳

God could not be everywhere and therefore he made mothers. *–Jewish Proverb*

✳

What is home without a mother? *–Alice Hawthorne*

✳

The hand that rocks the cradle rules the world *–W.S. Ross*

✳

NATION

A nation's work never ends. Men may come and go, generations may pass but the life of a nation goes on. *–Jawaharlal Nehru*

✳

A nation reveals itself not only by the men it produces, but also by the men it honours, the men it remembers. *–John F. Kennedy*

✳

Nations get as good or as bad a government as they deserve. *–Allen Hume*

✳

The worth of a state, in the long run, is the worth of the individuals composing it. *–John Stewart Mill*

✷

NATURE

Nature speaks through our instincts very clearly, if only we listen to her. *–Mahatma Gandhi*

✷

Nature is a volume of which God is the author.

–Harvey

✷

All are but parts of one stupendous whole, whose body nature is, and God the soul. *–Pope*

✷

For use almost can change
the stamp of nature
And either curb the devil,
or throw him out
with wondrous potency. *–Shakespeare*

✷

GREED

The earth provides enough to satisfy every man's need but not for every man's greed. *–Mahatma Gandhi*

✷

NIGHT

Night's darkness is a bag that bursts with the gold of the dawn. *–Rabindranath Tagore*

✷

Nearer the dawn, the darker the night. *–Longfellow*

*

Night is the blotting paper of many sorrows.

–Litaniseh

*

NIRVANA

The destruction of craving is nirvana

–Gautama Buddha

*

Health is the greatest acquisition, contentment, the greatest wealth, confidence, the best of relationships and nirvana, the highest happiness.

–Gautama Buddha

*

NON-VIOLENCE

The kingdom of Heaven is Ahimsa.

Non-violence is not a cover for cowardice, but it is the supreme virtue of the brave.

There is no such thing as defeat or despair in the dictionary of a man who bases his life on truth and ashimsa. *–Mahatma Gandhi*

*

OBJECTIONS

Nothing will ever be attempted if all possible objections must be first overcome. *–Dr. Johnson*

*

OFFENCE

When any one has offended me, I try to raise my soul so high that the offence cannot reach it.

–Descartes

✳

OPPORTUNITY

There is a tide in the affairs of men, which, taken at the flood, leads on to fortune. *–Shakespeare*

✳

We must beat the iron while it is hot; but we may polish it at leisure. *–Dryden*

✳

For every day I stand outside your door
And bid you wake, and rise to fight and win.

–Walter Malone

✳

OPTIMIST

Every day is a new birth in time, holding out new beginnings, new possibilities, new achievements. It holds out new hopes, new opportunities to all. In it you can become a new man, a new woman. From the whole past with its mistakes, failures and sorrows, you can rise a new being endued with power and purpose and radiant with the inspiration of a new ideal. *–Anon*

✳

An optimist sees an opportunity in every calamity; a pessimist sees a calamity in every opportunity.

–Anon

✳

A habit of looking at the best side of events is worth than a thousand pounds a year. *–Dr. Johnson*

✳

A pessimist thinks he is taking a chance, but the optimist thinks he is grasping an opportunity.

–Anon

✳

PATIENCE

To be patient under rebuke, and to appear so requires very distinct acts of self-control. *–Anon*

✳

Patience and perseverance overcome mountains.

–Mahatma Gandhi

✳

God is with the patient. *–Koran*

✳

Beware the fury of a patient man. *–Dryden*

✳

Patience is the key to contentment.

–Prophet Mohammad

✳

Our patience will achieve more than our force.

–Burke

✳

Patience is the art of hoping. *–Anon*

*

PATRIOTISM

I like to see a man proud of his country, and I like to see him so live that his country is proud of him.
–Abraham Lincoln

*

Patriotism is not a short and frenzied outburst of emotion, but the tranquil and steady dedication of a lifetime. *–Adlai Stevenson*

*

Patriotism is not enough. I must have no hatred or bitterness towards anyone. *–Edith Cavell*

*

PEACE

Peace cannot be purchased by compromise with evil or surrender to it. *–Jawaharlal Nehru*

*

We cannot seek peace in the language of wars and threats. *–Jawaharlal Nehru*

*

Peace is not in the heart of the carnal man, nor in the man who is devoted to outward things, but in the fervent spiritual man. *–Thomas A. Kempis*

*

The more you sweat in peace, the less you bleed in war. *–Hyman Rickover*

✳

Peace hath her victories no less renowned than war. *–Milton*

✳

PEOPLE

Types of People:

The Synthesist
The Idealist
The Pragmatist
The Realist
The Analyst. *–Anon*

✳

The Lord prefers common-looking people. That is the reason He made so many of them.

–Abraham Lincoln

✳

The voice of the people is the voice of God.

–Latin Saying

✳

PERFORMANCE

In the last analysis, management is practice. Its essence is not knowledge but doing. Its test is not logic, but results. Its only authority is performance.

–Peter Drucker

✳

Performance must therefore be under constant review, so that corrective actions are taken immediately. *–K.N. Tamja*

✳

PERSEVERANCE

Nothing in the world can take the place of persistence. Talent will not. Nothing is more common than unsuccessful men with talent. Genius will not; unrewarded genius is almost a proverb. Education will not; the world is full of educated derilicts. Persistence and determination alone are omnipotent. The slogan, "Press on" has solved and will always solve the problems of the human race.

–Calvin Coolidge

All the performance of human art at which we look with praise and wonder, are instances of the restless forces of perseverance. It is by this that the quarry becomes a pyramid, and that distant countries are united with canals. If a man was to compare the effect of a single stroke of the pick-axe or of one impression of the spade with the general design and last result, he would be overwhelmed by the sense of their proportion. Yet those petty operations incessantly continued, in time surmount the greatest difficulties and mountains are levelled, and oceans bounded by the slender force of human beings. *–Dr. Johnson*

✳

Perseverance is not a long race; it is many short races one after another. *–Walter Elliot*

✳

We can do anything we want to do if we stick to it long enough. *–Helen Keller*

✳

Quitting is easy, fighting is hard. Quitting is losing, fighting is winning. *–Buck Nystrom*

✳

PHILOSOPHY

To be philosophical is not merely to have subtle thoughts, nor either to found a school, but so to love wisdom as to live according to its dictates, a life of simplicity, magnanimity and trust.

–Henry David Thoreau

✳

Philosophy is the art of living. *–Plutarch*

✳

The subject of philosophy, which is not primarily utilitarian in its aims, is a great instrument of liberal education. Its aim is one of elevating man above worldliness, of making him superior to circumstances, of liberating him from the thrall of material things.

Philosophy claims to implant in the minds of those, who are of a nature to profit by its teachings and influence, a taste for those things which the world cannot give and cannot take away.

If properly pursued, it arms us against sorrow and calamity, against boredom and discouragement.

It may not, perhaps, prepare us for success, if we mean by it material wealth. But it helps us to love those aims and ideals, the things beyond all price, on which the generality of men, who aim at success, do not set their hearts.
To Form Men is the Object of Philosophy.

–Dr. S. Radhakrishnan

✳

PLEASURE

Sweet is pleasure after pain. *–Dryden*

✳

Everything that depends on others gives pain; everything that depends on ourself gives pleasure.

–Manu

✳

POLITENESS

True politeness is perfect ease and freedom. It simply consists of treating others just as you love to be treated yourself. *–Samuel Smiles*

✳

POOR

It is not the man who has too little, but the man who craves for more that is poor. *–Seneca*

✳

POLITICS

Politics in general, both of parties and of nations, would appear to be the human activity in which error is most common because reason is least esteemed.

–Vincent Sheen

✳

POVERTY

The greatest of evils and the worst of crimes—poverty. *–Bernard Shaw*

✳

To be poor and independent is very nearly an impossibility. *–William Cobbet*

✳

The greatest man in history was the poorest.

–Emerson

✳

Poverty is no vice, but an inconvenience.

–John Florio

✳

POWER

Power corrupts, absolute power corrupts absolutely.

–Lord Acton

✳

Power comes from sincere service.

–Mahatma Gandhi

✳

PRAYER

My words fly up, my thoughts remain below, words without thought never to heaven go. *–Shakespeare*

✳

Father of light and life,
Thou God Supreme!
Oh, teach me what is good, teach me thyself,
Save me from folly, vanity and vice,
From every low pursuit; and fill my soul
With knowledge, conscious peace and virtue pure;
Sacred, substantial never fading bliss.

–Thompson's Poems

✳

If you begin to live life looking for the God that is all around you, every moment becomes a prayer.

–Frank Bianco

✳

An hour's contemplation and study of God's creation is better than a year of adoration. *–Koran*

✳

Prayer has saved my life; without it I should have been a raving lunatic. Prayer must be the very core of the life of man. The spirit becomes unclean if the heart is not washed by prayer.

It is better in prayer to have a heart without words than word without a heart. *–Mahatma Gandhi*

✳

Who rises from prayer a better man, his prayer is answered. *–George Meredith*

✳

Prayer is not asking. It is a longing of the soul. *–Mahatma Gandhi*

✳

Prayer is the voice of faith. *–Horne*

✳

Lord, make me an instrument of thy peace. Wherever there is hatred, let me sow love; where there is doubt, faith; where there is despair, hope; where there is darkness, light; and where there is sadness, joy.

Oh, divine master, grant that I do not seek so much to be consoled as to console; to be understood as to understand, to be loved as to love. For it is in giving that we receive, it is in pardoning that we are pardoned, and it is in dying that we are born to everlasting life. *–St. Francis of Assissi*

✳

PREJUDICE

Preconceived notions are the locks on the door to wisdom. *–Merry Browne*

✳

Our prejudices are our mistresses, reason is at best our wife, very often heard indeed but seldom minded. *–Lord Chesterton*

✳

Prejudice is the child of ignorance. *–Hazlitt*

✳

It is never too late to give up your prejudices.

–Henry David Thoreau

✳

PRETENCE

Those who pretend to know what they do not, will be thought ignorant of even what they know.

–Thiruvalluvar

✳

THE PRESENT MOMENT

He who governed the world before I was born, shall take care of it likewise when I am dead. My part is to improve the present moment. *–Anon*

✳

Whatever you can do, or dream you can, begin it. Boldness has genius, power and magic in it. Begin it, Now. *–Goethe*

✳

If a person does not enjoy good fortune when he has it, then he should not complain when it is gone.

–Cervantes

✳

PRICE

Every prize has its price. The prize is yes; the price is no. *–Anon*

✳

For anything worth having, one must pay the price; and the price is always work, patience, love, self-sacrifice—no paper currency, no promises to pay, but the gold of real service. *–John Burroughs*

✳

If you want something different from what you have, you must pay the price of becoming something different from what you are. *–Edward M. Hager*

✳

Who is a cynic? A man who knows the price of everything and the value of nothing. *–Oscar Wilde*

✳

Fortune is like the market, where many times, if you can stay a little, the price will fall. *–Francis Bacon*

✳

PRINCIPLE

Principle is a passion for truth. *–Hazlitt*

✳

A precedent embalms a principle. *–Disraeli*

✳

Principles become modified in practice by facts. *–Cooper*

✳

PRIVATE ENTERPRISE

If private enterprise had not begotten the richest world that ever existed, there would have been much less for the welfare state to distribute. *–G. Garrel*

✳

Never cheapen the product. Never cheapen the wage. Never overcharge the public. Put brains into the method. The new method must produce the profit.

–Henry Ford

✳

PROCRASTINATION

Know the true value of time. Snatch, seize and enjoy every moment of it. No idleness, no laziness, no procrastination; never put off till tomorrow what you can do today. *–Chesterfield*

✳

Procrastination is the thief of time. *–Edward Young*

✳

PROGRESS

All change is not progress. All knowledge is not wisdom. *–Abraham Lincoln*

✳

Progress is the activity of today and assurance of tomorrow. *–Emerson*

✳

Progress is a lame woman. It can only come hopping.

–Mahatma Gandhi

✳

Progress is the law of life, man is not man yet.

–Browning

✳

PROMISE

It is great to show promise; it is tragic not to fulfil it.

–Charles Moore

✳

We promise according to our hopes, and perform according to our fears. *–La Rochefoucauld*

✳

He who is the most slow in making a promise is the most faithful in the performance of it. *–Rousseau*

✳

PROSPERITY

When prosperity comes, do not use all of it.

–Confucius

✳

Prosperity makes some friends and many enemies.

–Anon

✳

You cannot bring about prosperity by discouraging thrift. *–Abraham Lincoln*

✳

Prosperity doth best discover vice; but adversity doth discover virtue. *–Bacon*

✳

PURPOSE

Whether the hand holds a broom or a pen, it has nothing to do with the value of the work accomplished. It is the use to which the tool is turned, the purpose that is put into it, that makes it worthwhile or worthless. *–Anon*

READING

Reading is to the mind what exercise is to the body. *–Joseph Addison*

The love of reading enables a man to exchange the wearisome hours of life which come to everyone for hours of delight. *–Montesquieu*

*

Resolve to edge in a little reading every day. If you gain but 15 minutes a day, it will make itself felt at the end of the year. *–Horace Mann*

*

Reading maketh a full man; conference a ready man, and writing an exact man. *–Bacon*

*

RATIONALISM

Rationalism is a hideous monster when it claims for itself omnipotence. *–Mahatma Gandhi*

REFORM

Reform must come from within, not from without. You cannot legislate virtue. *–Gibbon*

✳

To innovate is not reform. *–Burke*

✳

RELATIONSHIP

A relationship is like a diamond, which has to be cut and polished to enhance its lustre and beauty.

–Rabindranath Tagore

✳

RELIGION

He only can be happy who, having a religion, knows what it rightly demands of him. *–Anon*

✳

Religion is not a theory of God. It is spiritual consciousness. *–Dr. S. Radhakrishnan*

✳

Think true, like love—they constitute the essence of religion. *–Dr. S. Radhakrishnan*

✳

Like the bee gathering honey from different flowers, the wise man accepts the essence of different scriptures and sees only the good in all religions.

–Srimad Bhagavatam

✳

Love of God and love of neighbour are the two sides, inward and outward, of a truly religious soul.

–Dr. S. Radhakrishnan

✻

Religion is force of belief cleansing the inward parts. For this reason, the primary religious virtue is sincerity, a penetrating sincerity.

Religion is the art and theory of the internal life of man. *–A.N. Whitehead*

✻

Religion is the technique of perfect living, of gaining a better mastery over oneself.

–Swami Chinmayananda

✻

All religions are true, God can be reached by different religions. Many rivers flow by many ways but they all enter the sea. They are all one. *–Sri Ramakrishna*

✻

REMORSE

Of all sad words of tongue or pen, the saddest are these: "It might have been." *–Whittier*

✻

Repentance is the attempt of the inner man to return home after a wonderful night out. *–Hans Clarin*

✻

Hearty repentance breaks the edge of guilt and leads the way to a proper understanding.

–Mahatma Gandhi

✳

He who dares to say has always to repent afterwards.

–Guru Nanak

✳

RESPONSIBILITY

Rank does not confer privilege or give power. It imposes responsibility. *–Peter Drucker*

✳

RETRIBUTION

Nothing can work me damage except myself. The harm that I sustain I carry about me and never am a real sufferer but by my own fault. *–St. Bernard*

✳

He that diggeth a pit shall fall into it.

–Old Testament

✳

Whatsoever a man soweth, that shall he also reap. *–New Testament*

✳

RETROSPECTION

When one thinks of all one might have done, and all

one ought to have done, there seems to be no time left to think of wrongs we have received or benefits we have missed. *–Benjamin Jowett*

✳

REVOLUTION

Those who make peaceful revolution impossible, make violent revolution inevitable. *–J.F. Kennedy*

✳

Every revolution was first a thought in one man's mind. *–Emerson*

✳

RICHES

Man is rich with little were his judgements true; Nature is frugal and her wants are few. *–Anon*

✳

A man is rich in proportion to the number of things he can do without. *–Thoreau*

✳

Riches are a good handmaid, but a bad mistress. *–Bacon*

✳

RIDICULE

Give up the awful disease that is creeping into our national blood, that idea of ridiculing everything. *–Swami Vivekananda*

✳

RIGHT AND WRONG

Be sure you are right, then go ahead.

–David Crockett

✳

Two wrongs can never make a right.

–English Proverb

✳

When we know that life will go on without serious break through endless years, it puts a new meaning into every noble and worthy beginning. Every right and good thing, however small it may seem, shall live for ever. *–Anon*

✳

Perhaps it is better to be irresponsible and right than responsible and wrong. *–Anon*

✳

One truth is clear, it is whatever is right. *–Pope*

✳

SACRIFICE

No sacrifice is worth the name unless it is a joy.

–Mahatma Gandhi

✳

Sacrifice and a long face go ill together.

–Mahatma Gandhi

✳

Good manners are made up of petty sacrifices

–Emerson

✳

SATISFACTION

On the shores of success rises the sun of satisfaction.

–Anon

✷

SCIENCE

Science is both knowledge and power. It has interest as well as utility. It is illuminating as well as fruitful.

–Dr. S. Radhakrishnan

✷

Science is organised knowledge. *–Herbert Spencer*

✷

When Science from Creation's face
Enchantment's veil withdraws,
What lovely visions yield their place
To cold material laws. *–Thomas Campbell*

✷

Science is the art of knowing. Art is the science of feeling. *–C. Caudwell*

✷

SELF-IMAGE

A strong, positive self-image is the best possible preparation for success in life. *–Dr. Joyce Brothers*

✷

SELF-LAUDATION

Self-laudation abounds among the unpolished, but

nothing can stamp a man more sharply as ill bred.

–Charles Buxton

✳

SELF-RELIANCE

No one saves us but ourselves. No one can and no one may. Others only point the path, we ourselves must walk the way. *–Anon*

✳

SELF-REFORM

A man who reforms himself has contributed his full share towards the reformation of his neighbour.

–Norman Douglas

✳

If there is to be any regeneration of our people, it must take place in the small laboratories of our private lives. We must realise with all the intensity we can command, that refashioning our own character is not only the most satisfying and rewarding preoccupation of man, but it is also the most important contribution we can make to society. *–Dr. Alexis Carrel*

✳

The highest patriotism and philanthropy consists, not so much in altering laws and modifying institutions, as in helping and stimulating men and women to elevate and improve themselves by their own free and independent individual action. *–Samuel Smiles*

✳

One should lift oneself by one's own efforts and should not degrade oneself. For one's own self is one's friend as also one's enemy.

One's own self is the friend by whom one's lower self (mind and its tendency to degrade) has been conquered. Even so, one's very self of him who has not conquered his lower self behaves antagonistically like an enemy. *–Bhagavat Gita*

*

SELF-CONTROL

Just stand aside and watch yourself go by. Think of yourself as 'he' instead of 'I'. *–Strickland Gillilan*

*

The self-restrained seldom err. *–Confucius*

*

Know the self to be the master, the body to be the chariot, intellect the charioteer, the mind the reins, the sense organs the horses, sense objects the pathways.

A man of understanding who controls his mind and senses is like a charioteer with tamed horses. One who lacks understanding and does not control his mind and senses is like a charioteer with wild horses.

–Kathopanishad

When any fit of anxiety, or gloominess, or perversion of mind lays hold upon you, make it a rule not to publish it by complaints, but exert your whole care to hide it; by endeavouring to hide it, you will drive it away. Be always busy. *–Dr. Johnson*

✳

Self-control is only courage under another form.

–Samuel Smiles

✳

SERVICE

Confucius wrote: "He who wishes to secure the good of others, has already secured his own". There is a direct link between service to others and rewards in life. *–Ari Kiev, M.D.*

✳

This body is for service to others. *–Kalidasa*

✳

Service can have no meaning unless one takes pleasure in it. When it is done for show or for fear of public opinion, it stunts the man and crushes his spirit.

–Mahatma Gandhi

✳

The service we render others is really the rent we pay for our room on this earth. *–Wilfred Grenfell*

✳

SHARE

The miracle is this—the more we share, the more we have. *–Leonard Nimoy*

✳

SILENCE

God's silence ripens man's thoughts into speech.
–Rabindranath Tagore

✳

Silence is golden, speech is silvern. *–Proverb*

✳

Silence is the element in which great things fashion themselves. *–Carlyle*

✳

Silence is of eternity, speech is of time. *–Carlyle*

✳

SILVER LINING

There was never a cloud so heavy and black.
That it had not a silver lining.
There was never a night so dreary and dark.
That the stars were not somewhere shining. *–Anon*

✳

SIN

It is a great liberty to be able not to sin. It is the greatest liberty to be unable to sin. *–St. Augustine*

✳

Just as iron rust accumulates and self-born, eats ifself away, so with the man who sinneth, day by day . His own deeds to destruction lead him on.

–Gautam Buddha

*

SMART MEN

Smart men put up with small annoyances to gain larger rewards later. *–Anon*

*

SMILE

'Tis easy enough to be pleasant when life flows along like a song; but the man worthwhile is the one who will smile when everything goes dead wrong.

–Ella W. Wilcox

*

It creates sunshine in the home fosters goodwill in business. It is the best antidote for trouble. And yet it cannot be begged, borrowed or stolen, for it is no value unless it is freely given away. *–Anon*

*

A man without a smiling face must not open a shop.

–Chinese Proverb

*

SOLITUDE

It is easy in the world to live after the world's opinion; it is easy in solitude to live after one's own opinion; but the great man is he who, in the midst of the crowd, keeps with perfect sweetness, the independence of solitude. *–Emerson*

✳

When from our better selves we have too long been parted by the hurrying world and droop, sick of its business, of its pleasures tired, how gracious, how benign, is solitude! *–Wordsworth*

✳

SPEECH

Speech is civilization itself. The word, even the most contradictory word, preserves contact—it is silence which isolates. *–Thomas Mann*

✳

Darts, barbed arrow, iron-headed spears, however deep they penetrate the flesh, may be extracted, but a cutting speech that pierces like a javelin to the heart, none can remove; it lies and rankles there.

–Mahabharata

✳

SPIRITUAL ORIENTATION

What the world requires today is spiritual orientation. The redemption of the human race as a whole is the goal of human history which can happen if each individual exerts himself, puts himself to all sorts of exercises and understands what true religion is.

–Dr. S. Radhakrishnan

✳

To be spiritual is not to reject reason, but to go beyond it. *–Dr. S. Radhakrishnan*

✳

STRENGTH

Strength of numbers is the delight of the timid. The valiant of spirit glory in fighting alone.

–Mahatma Gandhi

✳

O, it is excellent to have a giant's strength; but it is tyrannous to use it like a giant. *–Shakespeare*

✳

STUPIDITY

I shall not commit the fashionable stupidity of regarding everything I can't explain as fraud.

–Carl Jung

✳

SUCCESS

Nothing succeeds like success. *–Talleyrand*

✳

No man deserves success unless his success benefits others as well as himself. *–Anon*

✳

Measure success not by what you have done, but what you could do. *–Barbara Hatcher*

✳

There aren't any rules for success that work unless you do. *–Anon*

✳

Rest if you must—but never quit. You may succeed with one more blow. Success is failure turned inside out—The silver tint of the clouds of doubt—and you never can tell how close you are. It may be near when it seems afar; so stick to the fight when you are hardest hit. It's when things seem worst that *you must not quit.* *–Anon*

✳

Facing it—always facing it—that is the way to get through. *–Joseph Conrad*

✳

There is no defeat except from within. There is really no insurmountable barrier, except your own inherent weakness of purpose. *–Emerson*

✳

The secret of success in life is for a man to be ready for his opportunity when it comes.

–Benjamin Disraeli

✳

Coming together is a beginning; keeping together is progress and working together is success.

–Henry Ford

I know of no more encouraging a fact than the unquestionable ability of man to elevate his life by a conscious endeavour. If one advances confidently in the direction of his dreams, and endeavours to live the life he has imagined, he will meet with a success unexpected in common hours.

–Henry David Thoreau

*

The wise say that unlimited enthusiasm, efficiency and refusal to accept defeat are the virtues that lead to sure success in any venture. *–Ramayana*

*

Work hard. It is not always a popular concept today, but it is an effective one. The very fact that we live in a work-shy age means that the dynamic, energetic person can more easily make his way towards the success he seeks. *–Anon*

*

TALENT

If you have great talents, industry will improve them; if you have but moderate abilities, industry will supply their deficiency. *–Sir Joshua Reynolds*

*

TEACHER

Woe to the teacher who teaches one thing with his lips, and carries another in his breast.

–Mahatma Gandhi

If you would thoroughly know anything, teach it to others. *–Tryon Edwards*

✳

No one was ever really taught by another; each of us has to teach himself. *–Swami Vivekananda*

✳

A teacher affects eternity; he can never tell where his influence stops. *–Henry Adams*

✳

TEMPER

Temper is a funny thing; you can't get rid of it by losing it. *–Somerset Maugham*

✳

TEMPTATION

Temptations are like tramps; treat one well and he will return with his friends! *–M. M.*

✳

Lead us not into temptation, but deliver us from evil. *–Bible*

✳

THOUGHTS

All truly wise thoughts have been thought already thousands of times; but to make them truly ours, we must think them over again honestly, until they take root in our personal experience. *–Goethe*

✳

Thought takes man out of servitude. *–Emerson*

✳

All the actions that we see in the world, all the movements in human society, all the works that we have around us, are simply the display of thought, the manifestation of the will of man.

–Swami Vivekananda

✳

Every word, every thought, shapes the mind and without understanding every thought, mind becomes a slave to words and sorrow begins.

–Jiddu Krishnamurthy

✳

There is nothing either good or bad, but thinking makes it so. *–Shakespeare*

✳

Thought without action is an abortion; action without thought is folly. *–Jawaharlal Nehru*

✳

TIME

A day once gone will never return. Therefore, one should be diligent each moment to do good. We reach the goal of good life by pious work. *–Mahavira*

✳

For everything there is a season, and a time to every purpose under the heaven: a time to be born, and a time to die; a time to plant and a time to pluck that which is planted. *–Bible*

✳

TODAY AND TOMORROW

The poison of panic grows in 'yesterdays'. The flower of felicity grows in 'tomorrows'. Make all your 'tomorrows' happy 'todays', so that your life will be long and healthy, successful and vital.

–Walter M. Germain

✳

Build today, then, strong and sure, with a firm and ample base. And ascending and secure shall tomorrow find its place. *–Longfellow*

✳

TRANQUILITY

The unthinking man can have no peace, and how can there be happiness for one lacking in tranquility ?

–Bhagavat Gita

✳

TRUST

To be trusted is a greater compliment than to be loved.

–J. Macdonald

✳

The only way to make a man trustworthy is to trust him. *–Henry Stimson*

✳

TRUTH, AND FALSE

He is true in the truest sense of the word who is true in thought, word and deed. *–Koran*

✳

Truth can be sweet or bitter, but it can never be bad. A lie can be sweet or bitter, but it can never be good.

–Constance Vigil

✳

It is a poor mind that will think with the multitude. Truth is not altered by the opinion of the vulgar or the confirmation of the many. *–Giordano Bruno*

✳

If you tell the truth, you don't have to remember anything. *–Mark Twain*

✳

For truth is truth to the end of reckoning.

–Shakespeare

✳

This above all—to thine own self be true;
And it must follow, as the night the day,
Thou canst not then be false to any man.

–Shakespeare

✳

I know no diplomacy save that of truth.

–Mahatma Gandhi

✳

Truth is the golden girdle of the globe. *–Cowper*

✳

You shall know the truth, and the truth shall make you free. *–Bible*

✳

NOT TRYING

There is no comparison between that which is lost by not succeeding and that which is lost by not trying.

–Bacon

✳

USELESS

Nothing useless is, or low,
Each thing in its place is best;
And what seems but idle show,
Strengthens and supports the rest. *–Longfellow*

✳

VICTORY

I found the task that I dreaded so,
Was not so difficult when once begun.
It was the dread itself that was the foe;
And dread once conquered means a victory won.

–Margaret E. Brunner

✳

Victory over oneself is indeed better than victory over others; not even a God could change into defeat the victory of a man who has vanquished himself.

–Gautama Buddha

✳

O death, where is thy sting ? O grave, where is thy victory ? *–Bible*

✳

VIOLENCE

I shall rather have violence than cowardice masquerading as non-violence. *–Mahatma Gandhi*

✳

These violent delights have violent ends, and in their triumph die. *–Shakespeare*

✳

VIRTUE

Virtue consists not in abstaining from vice, but not desiring it. *–Bernard Shaw*

✳

Virtue is an angel, but she is a blind one, and must ask of knowledge to show her the pathway that leads to her goal. *–Horace Mann*

✳

Only a sweet and virtuous soul, like seasoned timber, never gives. But when the whole world turns to coal, then chiefly lives. *–George Herbert*

✳

Virtue is its own reward. *–Cicero*

✳

It is virtue, and not birth, that makes us noble. Great actions speak great minds, and such should govern. *–John Fletcher*

✳

Know then this truth (enough for men to know)
"Virtue alone is happiness below." *–Pope*

✳

Virtue is the denial of self and response to what is right and proper. *–Confucius*

✳

VISION

Nothing ever built arose to touch the skies unless someone dreamed that it should, believed that it could and someone willed that it must. *–Dr. A. Schweitzer*

✳

Where there is no vision, people perish. *–Bible*

✳

For I dipt into the future, far as human eye could see,
Saw the vision of the world, and all the wonder that would be. *–Tennyson*

✳

WAR AND PEACE

War is the negation of truth and humanity.

–Jawaharlal Nehru

✳

There never was a good war or a bad peace.

–Benjamin Franklin

✳

War is the science of destruction. *–John S.C. Abbot*

✳

WEALTH

Without a rich heart, wealth is a poor beggar.

–Emerson

✳

WISDOM

Science at best is not wisdom; it is knowledge. Wisdom is knowledge with judgement.

–Lord Calder

✳

Commonsense in an uncommon degree is what the world calls wisdom. *–S.T. Coleridge*

✳

Abundance of knowledge does not teach men to be wise. *–Heraclitus*

✳

Be civil to all; sociable to many; familiar with few; friend to one; enemy to none. *–Benjamin Franklin*

✳

WORDS

A very great part of the mischiefs that vex the world arises from words. *–Burke*

✳

Words should be scattered like seeds, no matter how small the seed may be; if it has once found favourable ground, it unfolds its strength. *–Seneca*

✳

In the beginning was the Word, and the Word was with God, and the Word was God. *–Bible*

✳

WORK

Blessed is he who has found his work; let him ask no other happiness. *–Carlyle*

✳

It is only by labour that thought can be made healthy, and only by good thought that labour can be made happy; and the two cannot be separated with impunity. *–Anon*

✳

Do your work—not just your work and no more, but a little more for the lavishing's sake; that little more which is worth all the rest, and if you suffer as you must, and if you doubt as you must, do your work.

Put your heart into it and the sky will clear.

–Dean Farrar

✳

With malice towards none, with charity for all, with firmness in the right as God gives us to see the right, let us finish the work we are in. *–Abraham Lincoln*

✳

Work is a secular form of sanctity

–Dr. S. Radhakrishnan

✳

Work is worship. *–Proverb*

✳

Far and away the best prize that life offers is the chance to work hard at work worth doing.

–Theodore Roosevelt

✳

When work is a pleasure, life is a joy! When work is a duty, life is slavery. *–Maxim Gorky*

✳

If you wonder how to do a job, get started, and wonder how you did it! *–Goethe*

✳

WORSHIP

The leaf becomes flower when it loves. The flower becomes fruit when it worships.

–Rabindranath Tagore

✳

WRONG

Every piece of wrongdoing strikes a blow at our own heart. When taking a mean advantage, people too easily forget that they do themselves more injury than others. *–Joseph Parker*

✳

Wrong cannot afford defeat but right can.

–Rabindranath Tagore

✳

YOGA

Equipoise is said to be yoga. Also equivision is yoga. Yoga is adeptness in work too. *–Bhagavat Gita*

✳

Yoga is getting to God, relating oneself to the Power that rules the universe, touching the Absolute. It is the yoking not merely this or that power of the soul, but all the forces of heart, mind and will to God.

–Dr. S. Radhakrishnan

✳

ZEAL

Our offerings please God according to our zeal and not according to their value. *–Salvianus*

✳

Labour with what zeal we will, something still remains undone. *–Longfellow*

✳